A Call To Arms

An Introduction of the Case for Christian Activism in Our Government

By: Tommy Dimsdale

Table of Contents:

<u>Dedicated to:</u>

This book is dedicated to those who fought and died for our freedom. Without their sacrifice the world would have been denied the awe of the American experiment. Without the constant spilling of blood, shed for our sake, none of us would have the right to seek change in our government, run for office or even worship God as we please. Through this book I hope to instill the kind of action that ensures that the lives lost here and abroad were not lost in vain. Thank you to those who have given up so much for our liberty. May posterity hold a special chapter in history for you.

<u>Foreword</u>

A Call To Arms is a must read for America! These insights and inspirations will truly open your eyes to both how blessed we are to be Americans and how we can stand together in an ever changing and challenging time in history. I encourage you to take time to not only thoroughly read this book but to really ponder the power and exceptionalism of our beloved country. Moreover, this book will open your eyes to the reality and truth that each of us can make a difference not just for today, but for the generations to follow. It is a wonderful reminder of how much blood, sweat, tears, and prayers were lifted up on our behalf over two centuries ago when our country was founded! There is no reason we cannot achieve the same greatness tomorrow that our founders did yesterday! If America is going to endure for future generations, we are going to have to take a stand and refuse to let the same freedom so many have given their lives for be taken away. In reading this book, I am more energized and encouraged than ever before as it has really helped me realize that victory comes at great cost, freedom is too precious to be lost, and life, liberty, and the pursuit of happiness are more than just words!

Whenever our memories outnumber our dreams we are destined to die as a nation. Thank you, Tommy, for pouring your passion into every page and know that this book will set the stage for real change to begin in America! O.K. Americans...Arise and make a difference! Get involved in your destiny!

Hosea 4:6 "My people are destroyed for lack of knowledge"

Dr. Gregory A. Butler

__Introduction:__

Navigating the waters of politics, religion and history I've found myself wondering why Christians do not get involved in politics as they did back in the days of our nation's founding. If only they knew how our ancestors had lived! If only they realized just how right they are that we were born a Christian nation, maybe then they would be inspired to jump aboard a campaign or advocacy group! To dive into the reasons behind our convictions is truly a rewarding experience and I'm glad you've taken the time to pick up this book and see for yourself just how our nation was brought out of the hands of tyranny and into the light of God's blessings! The moment for action is now and the longer I stay engaged the more optimistic I am of Christian influence in today's political realm. We're just starting to see the rewards of this activism. It has been a struggle in the past, however.

Time after time, campaign after campaign, issue after issue I've found many Christians to be peculiarly apathetic to the pleas of activists on the front lines of conservatism. I have spent a good portion of my time in political activism toward trying to get volunteers or donors out in force to either support a conservative agenda or support a Godly man or woman to get into office, only to receive an attitude of passiveness from individuals who I thought would be excited to make a change. Many a phone call would end with the repetitive words "can't help but I'll pray for ya." This left the rest of my group of fellow patriots starving for badly needed support and working at a disadvantage to a liberal, corrupt and well-funded opponent. By the grace of God, we were able to win many battles, but some were by the skin of our teeth and left the volunteer force weary and worn out over rigorous campaigning and advocating.

Over several years of involvement, I began to see the need for Christian activism, but I had to figure out how to tap into that market of change. I'm still growing in my understanding of what drives people to action, what inspires them and what makes them feel a sense of purpose to go out and engage with their community. For myself, it was listening to the stories I was never told in school. The story of Washington shaking out his jacket to find 4 musket shot holes, inches away from his chest, and another in his hat, left me in awe of God's plan. The story of the siege of Yorktown where perfect Providential timing of the French fleet along with a powerful gale of storms in New York that left the British navy in tatters, shook me to my core. To hear the fervor and passion in the speeches of the founding fathers, submitting to God's righteous authority, convinced me that separation of church and state (as the courts have perceived it) was a lie. So, I've started laying out the evidence of our founding and I've found that Christians latch on to it. When teaching in front of youth groups, teen after teen have approached me in awe and surprise concerning the facts that their teachers won't tell them in public high school. Adults have approached me, excited to see the message being spread. So far, this has been a useful tool in recruiting youth and Christians alike to bringing our nation back to the Cross, the Constitution and Conservatism. I hope this book can also be a spring board for your activism, to inspire, captivate and move you to action in your local precinct, county and state.

"Our Constitution was made only for a moral and religious people. It is wholly inadequate to the government of any other."

– John Adams[1]

---

[1] Founders Online: From John Adams to Massachusetts Militia, 11 October 1798." National Archives and Records Administration, National Archives and Records Administration, founders.archives.gov/documents/Adams/99-02-02-3102.

Chapter 1
Christianity Under Fire

As Christians we've all heard the misquoted and misconstrued snippets about our founding fathers being agnostic or atheists. I want you to think to yourself, "if I were to be confronted about this, if I were to hear someone proclaiming our nation was built upon secularism, how would I respond?" For so long we as Christians have bought into Christianity and the following of Jesus Christ because it's all we've ever known. It's what dad believed, it's what grandpa believed, but most of us have never dug into WHY we believe WHAT we believe. The Bible tells us in I Peter 3:15 – "But in your hearts revere Christ as Lord. Always be prepared to give an answer to everyone who asks you to give the reason for the hope that you have. But do this with gentleness and respect." The Bible also states in II Timothy 4:2 – "Preach the word, be prepared in season and out of season; correct, rebuke and encourage- with great patience and careful instruction." God wanted us to know He was Lord not just because Grandad said so or because it's the social norm of our home town but because we honestly have facts to back up our faith, that we have a "reason for our hope." Even Thomas Jefferson realized this when he wrote a letter to his nephew, "Question with boldness even the existence of a God; because, if there is one, he must more approve of the homage of reason, than that of blindfolded fear."[2] Jefferson, a scholar of the Bible, knew that we must study and apply reason to our beliefs, and when we do, it only strengthens our faith.

Over time, the liberal left has repeatedly driven home the falsehood and misconception of the "separation of church and state" phrase, the supposed secularism of our founding fathers, and the omission of many great and wonderful stories that exalted God's glory in the time of the Revolution. They have seen success in the idea that if you repeat a lie often enough, people will believe you. Unfortunately, many pastors have come to believe the manipulation of the separation phrase and have passed that onto their congregations. Fears of losing a 501c3 status abound and deter any mention of Christian servitude in the political arena. Many churches are afraid to wade into the political waters for fear of losing their tax-exempt status, a

---

[2] "Jefferson Quotes & Family Letters." *Extract from Thomas Jefferson to Peter Carr, 10 Aug. 1787 [Quote] | Jefferson Quotes & Family Letters,* tjrs.monticello.org/letter/1297.

danger presented by the Johnson amendment, a measure
put forward by Lyndon B. Johnson and passed in 1954 to
ensure a win for his next presidential bid.[3] President
Trump signed an executive order weakening the Johnson
amendment during his first year in office.[4] However, to
completely eradicate the amendment, congress will have to
overturn it. As it sits at the time of this writing, the Senate
tax plan holds a provision to strike the amendment down,
allowing churches to weigh in on political matters but it
must be retained in the language of the bill after it exits
committee. No matter which way this goes, I will say that
the church will have much more to worry about than a
501c3 status if our nation continues to meander, unguided
by the salt and light of God's army. **Many Christians
would now resolve to believe these misconceptions and
begin to doubt the appropriateness of their involvement in
the civil arena and therefore, resolve to practice their faith
only within their homes and churches and not in public,
where it is so desperately needed.** Eighty million
evangelicals had the opportunity to vote in 2012, however
less than half of them, thirty-two million, decided to go
and make that difference ... less than half. We continue to
wonder why our nation is headed so far away from God

---

[3] Religion. "Its Time To Repeal The Johnson Amendment And Let Pastors Talk
Politics." The Federalist, 5 Dec. 2017, thefederalist.com/2017/12/01/time-repeal-
johnson-amendment-let-pastors-talk-politics/.
[4] Wagner, John, and Sarah Pulliam Bailey. "Trump signs order seeking to allow
churches to engage in more political activity." *The Washington Post*, WP
Company, 4 May 2017, www.washingtonpost.com/politics/trump-signs-order-
aimed-at-allowing-churches-to-engage-in-more-political-
activity/2017/05/04/024ed7c2-30d3-11e7-9534-
00e4656c22aa_story.html?utm_term=.dcc6d7c54d4f.

and why Christians are continually persecuted in the media. I'm here to tell you, we only have ourselves to blame. In these pages, we are going to discover how our founders were Christians, what they believed in and what they did to further that set of beliefs.

First, I want to set a tone of urgency for you. Even as I write these words, our freedoms in this country are growing increasingly narrow. Bit by bit they are being chiseled away. The reason? An apathetic view towards politics from the Christian populace. Let's look at a few examples of how Christians have been persecuted in the one nation that was supposed to champion those religious rights.

Kim Davis

I was entering an intermediate phase of activism when I saw on Fox News that a Kentucky clerk of court, Kim Davis, was being arrested for not handing out a marriage license to a gay couple that had come from out of state to stir up controversy for the LGBT community. Two homosexual men, David Ermold and David Moore, sued clerk of court, Kim Davis and the state of Kentucky when she refused to issue them a marriage license. Kim abstained from issuing the license because she would be violating her religious principles. Instead, the law was later changed in December 2015, which stated that the clerk of court did not have to sign off on such licenses, but that their deputies could.[5] This did not deter the couple from pursuing the case however. At the beginning of the fiasco, Kim Davis was arrested and spent several days in jail until she was able to reach out to a few conservative law makers and Matt Staver, chairman of the Liberty Council.[6] With their help, Kim was released but Kentucky taxpayers were still levied with a fine of more than $200,000 to pay for the homosexual couple's legal costs. This is America and yet we haven't the freedom to abstain from practices that violate our conscious when working in the public sector.

Coach Joe Kennedy

An ex-marine and high school football coach for Bremberton High in Washington, had made a habit of going out onto the football field before games and praying. Coach Kennedy would often be joined by his team on the field and sometimes the occasional parent. This was a practice he started in 2008 and for seven years everyone was supportive of Joe and his public display of Christianity. In 2015, an employee from another school district complained, claiming "separation of church and state" should prevent the coach from taking such action. In response, the school told the veteran coach that he could pray either in a secluded room or after every player and

---

[5] Press, Associated. "Kentucky bows to clerk Kim Davis and changes marriage license rules." *Los Angeles Times*, Los Angeles Times, 23 Dec. 2015, www.latimes.com/nation/nationnow/la-na-nn-kentucky-kim-davis-20151223-story.html.

[6] CBS/AP. "Kentucky clerk Kim Davis released from jail." *CBS News*, CBS Interactive, 8 Sept. 2015, www.cbsnews.com/news/kentucky-clerk-kim-davis-released-from-jail/.

parent had gone home. Essentially, the coach could pray only if no one could see him. Kennedy made an attempt to follow the rules and pray alone in the secluded room they had offered but God spoke to his heart and called on him to go back onto the field in defiance of the school's orders. When coach Joe Kennedy walked out onto the field and knelt to begin praying, he felt a presence around him. Upon ending his prayer, he looked up to survey not only his team, but the entire opposing team kneeled around him, also joining in prayer. After the game, the coach was released from his duties and terminated. Joe subsequently sued with the help of the First Liberty Institute of Plano, Texas. The opposing side, represented by attorney Richard Katskee from the Americans United for the Separation of Church and State group stated, "Teachers and coaches don't get to pressure students to pray."[7] Obviously, Joe Kennedy's actions had no act of coercion to force students or anyone else to pray, nor did it infringe on the true intent of the separation phrase, however we find ourselves in a nation where the government is not only non-supportive to Christianity but hostile to it and even Christians themselves.

Barronelle Stutzman

One more example leads to the story of Barronelle Stutzman, a 72-year-old, small business florist in

---

[7] Carter, Mike. "Appeals court refuses to reinstate Bremerton coach who prayed after games." *The Seattle Times,* The Seattle Times Company, 23 Aug. 2017, www.seattletimes.com/seattle-news/education/appeals-court-refuses-to-reinstate-bremerton-coach-who-prayed-at-games/.

Washington state. Baronelle had operated her store, Arlene's Flowers, for 30 years without thought or fear of government coercion against her religious convictions. One of her favorite customers, Rob Ingersoll, had been frequenting her floral shop for most of that time. Rob is a homosexual man but of course, Stutzman, being a true Christian began to hold a friendship with him. They would trade ideas for floral arrangements and shared an "artist's eye" for decoration. Barronelle cherished her friendship with him and sold to him on numerous occasions, even knowing that Rob was indeed gay. One day, Rob entered the floral shop with the news that he was getting married to another man and would like for Barronelle to provide flowers for the wedding. She politely declined, stating that her Christianity would not allow for her to provide for a wedding that went against her convictions. She proceeded to write down the name and number of another floral shop and seemingly, Rob went on his way. Somehow, the state of Washington found out about the exchange and immediately filed a law suit against Stutzman for running her business according to her faith. This lawsuit is still on going and is leaning towards a loss for Baronelle Stutzman, resulting in her paying hundreds of thousands of dollars in legal fees that the American Civil Liberties Union (ACLU) have racked up since the court case began in 2015. She stated, "They want my home, they want my finances, they want my personal business as an example for others to be quiet."[8]

Aaron & Melissa Klein

In January 2013, Rachel Bowman-Cryer accompanied her mother into Sweet Cakes, a local, family owned business in Oregon. She approached Melissa Klein, owner of the small business and asked if she would make a cake for her and her lesbian partner's wedding. Melissa politely declined, siting her religious convictions as grounds as to why she wouldn't feel comfortable making the cake and requested the couple find somewhere else that might could help.

Rachel sued the small business claiming the refusal inflicted "emotional damage" to them, likening the actions of the Kleins as "mental rape". The lesbian couple also blamed the bakery for their excessive weight claiming that the ordeal lead to a "loss of appetite" which somehow corresponded to "impaired digestion" and "weight gain".

Just recently the ruling went to the Oregon court of appeals in March of 2017 and was upheld in December the same year that the Christian bakery would be forced to pay

---

[8] Stutzman, Barronelle. "Why a friend is suing me: the Arlenes Flowers story." *The Seattle Times*, The Seattle Times Company, 12 Nov. 2015, www.seattletimes.com/opinion/why-a-good-friend-is-suing-me-the-arlenes-flowers-story/.

a fine of $135,000 to the gay couple, in restitution. [9] A fine of this magnitude will almost certainly put the couple out of business, destroying their current way of life and the hard work it took to start the venture. The message from the left is clear; "Comply, or we'll ruin you."

Fortunately, Christians have come to the aid of the Kleins but donating $109,000 to their GoFundMe page. Recently, the GoFundMe Company has removed them from the website and changed their rules of posting, just so it will not be a place for Christians in similar circumstances to go. Another pro-Christian site for fundraising, Continue to Give, has allowed the Kleins to continue to raise money. So far, they have broken the site's record for any single campaign, raising more than $350,000. This is wonderful news, but we can't lay back and think that the problem is solved. The Kleins live in constant fear that this same circumstance will return, and they will once again be in the same mess, along with many other Christian business owners. This is a cultural problem and it must change.

Since when has America turned into a society that openly persecutes Christians for displaying or practicing their faith? Since when have we, as a united community, continued to allow such twisting of the law to attack our fellow Christ followers? Our own inaction has led to the

---

[9] Coates, Erin. "Judge Issues a Final Ruling for 'Sweet Cakes' Owners Who Refused to Bake a Gay Wedding Cake." *The Western Journal*, 30 Dec. 2017, www.westernjournal.org/judge-issues-final-ruling-sweet-cakes-owners-refused-bake-gay-wedding-cake/.

current state of political affairs before us and there's only one entity to fix this: God's Church.

Chapter 2
The Case for Christian Activism

Once again, I strongly feel that stories and actual history can help bring Christians back to the realization that we were founded a Christian nation. There's tons of evidence, however we'll go over a few items in the next chapters and provide the foundation of the belief that our founders had a humble respect for God and Jesus Christ. We can always start with George Washington …

When we look to our nation's first president it's difficult to pick just one example of his Christian convictions, but let's start with his inauguration. On April 30th, 1789 Washington was sworn into office with his left hand on a copy of the 1767 King James Version Bible, opened to Genesis 49. At the end of Washington's oath, he then set the precedent to all other presidents after him, voluntarily adding the phrase, "so help me God" to the end of his oath. Washington, a man who many thought worthy of the authority of King, showed great respect for the Bible. Anyone who had done what he had done, sacrificed what he had sacrificed and come out victorious should have every reason to be boastful and proud. However, we see this larger than life character, the hand of guidance in an unstable and treacherous time, bow his large frame down to reverently kiss the pages of the Bible. How much more can a man do to prove to modern "historians" and college professors that he is, in fact, a Christian? Furthermore, he immediately turned and walked inside to the congressmen awaiting the first presidential address. Washington opened with a prayer, a long thought out and passionate prayer for his country. Washington wrote later, "it would be peculiarly improper to omit in this first official act my fervent supplications to that Almighty Being Who rules over the universe, Who presides in the councils of nations, and Whose providential aids can supply every human defect – that His benediction may consecrate to the liberties and happiness of the people of the United States a government instituted by themselves for these essential purposes."[10]

Washington's inaugural address was laced with religious and Christian sentiments referring to God. "No people can be bound to acknowledge and adore the Invisible Hand which conducts the affairs of men more than those of the United States. Every step by which they

---

[10] *National Archives and Records Administration*, National Archives and Records Administration, www.archives.gov/exhibits/american_originals/inaugtxt.html.

have advanced to the character of an independent nation seems to have been distinguished by some token of Providential Agency. . . [and] we ought to be no less persuaded that the propitious smiles of Heaven can never be expected on a nation that disregards the eternal rules of order and right which Heaven itself has ordained."[11] We can see from the documentation of proceedings that day that Washington led a large crowd from the Federal Hall to the St. Paul's Chapel where Reverend Samuel Provoost, an appointed chaplain of Congress, lead the delegation in prayers from Psalms 144-150, and asked God to bless the new government. Washington and the entire delegation remained for hours, praying for the birth of their new nation. So now we see, our nation's first presidential oath was carried out with a Bible, the phrase "so help me God", the kissing of the Bible from the most powerful man of the free world, an inaugural address referencing Christianity, a prayer, and a chapel service conducted by a federally appointed Chaplain. Yet we still have naysayers telling us that our nation was founded upon the idea of separation of church and state. Let's consider further evidences of our founder's convictions.

In 1787 the U.S. Congress finally approved the Constitution. In that same year the Northwest Ordinance was passed. The ordinance, reinforced the founder's beliefs that religion and morality should be taught in schools. It read as follows: *"Article 3: Religion, Morality and*

---

[11] *National Archives and Records Administration*, National Archives and Records Administration, www.archives.gov/exhibits/american_originals/inaugtxt.html.

Knowledge being necessary to good government and the happiness of mankind, schools and the means of education shall forever be encouraged."[12] This blatantly states that the purpose of a public-school system was to spread religion, morality and knowledge. Yet, the supreme Court condemns Christian school teachers who bring personal Bibles to school. They tear down the 10 commandments from the walls, remove school prayer, and any mention of Christ. All this is done in direct conflict with what the founders had envisioned for the future.

Washington later remarked on the Northwest Ordinance, *"Of all the dispositions and habits which lead to political prosperity, religion and morality are indispensable supports... and let us with caution indulge the supposition that morality can be maintained without religion...Reason and experience both forbid us to expect that national morality can prevail to the exclusion of religious principle. It is substantially true that virtue or morality is a spring of popular government."[13]* I revere how Washington recognized that religion must be coupled together with morality to have a sound society. For if we only have religion in society, we see the church wielding the sword of government, a highly unbiblical practice. We can see examples of this in the Roman Catholic church where churches could imprison people for not giving

---

[12] "Transcript of Northwest Ordinance (1787)." *Our Documents - Transcript of Northwest Ordinance (1787),* www.ourdocuments.gov/doc.php?flash=false&doc=8&page=transcript.
[13] *Avalon Project - Washington's Farewell Address 1796,* avalon.law.yale.edu/18th_century/washing.asp.

money to the church or worshipping in ways that were outside the parameters the church had set. This does not mean that the founders were hostile to Roman Catholics. After all, devoted Catholics such as Charles Carroll signed onto the Declaration of Independence and Thomas Fitzsummons and Daniel Carroll, also devoted Catholics, signed the Constitution. A multitude of Roman Catholic believers had integral parts to play in the battle for freedom. The founders did not hold contempt for any of these Catholics but merely acknowledged the shortcomings in the Roman Catholic ideas that the church should take on the role of the government.

Even though the First Amendment put a limit on the Federal government to prevent the establishment of religion, the states were free to do as they pleased. Numerous states, including my home state of South Carolina, held restrictions on anyone who did not believe in a holy deity from running for office. Many of these restrictions still stand today, and are still considered Constitutional practices. This may be confusing because the First Amendment does not allow an establishment of religion or a religious test to run for office. We have to remember that the Constitution was a *federal* document and was there to put limits on the *federal* government, not the states. Because the state government is more easily held accountable by the people, the Constitution holds very little authority over them. If a mistake is made, it can quickly be corrected, unlike a large lumbering federal government which takes time to fix problems. The founders saw that if a state wanted to establish a religion it could do so without impeding on the rights of an individual. That individual had more power to reverse that decision or to simply move to a state that better reflected his or her beliefs.

The states still understood that the ideas of any religious sect that required all power vested in the church, such as Islam or Roman Catholicism was inherently flawed. The framers of the Massachusetts Constitution wrote, *"We have… found ourselves obliged… to provide for the exclusion of these from offices who will not disclaim these principles of the spiritual jurisdiction which Roman Catholics in some centuries have held and which are subversive of a free government established by the people."[14]* In other words, if you didn't believe in the proper implementation of separation of church and state, they did not want you to run for office. A nation that only relied upon religion was doomed to steer towards tyranny. By excluding morality, the church could become corrupt and wield laws as a powerful tool unintended by God.

On the other hand, if we only have morality to steer a nation, then who decides what is moral if there's no guiding religion? This is exactly what we see today. In today's society it's a celebration of one's sexuality if they decide to be transgender or homosexual. Instead of issuing proper mental treatment and spiritual help, the society celebrates and encourages said behavior, all at the long-term detriment of the one being celebrated. Instead of the

---

[14] Barton, David. *Original Intent: the Courts, the Constitution, and Religion.* Wallbuilder Press 2000. Pg. 27

church being allowed to reach out and assist in this time of sexual confusion, the church is vilified as homophobes and bigots. This is the situation Washington warned of.

The purpose of the First Amendment will often be misconstrued. Liberals claim that this was a sure sign that the founders wanted nothing to do with religion and that it ought to be barred from entering the public square or political construct. The place where they get this wrong is called the "establishment clause". "Congress shall make no law respecting an establishment of religion or prohibiting the free exercise thereof…" Liberals have twisted the meaning of "establishment of religion" into an idea that must promote hostility towards religion, specifically Christianity. They view it to mean "any state assistance", when, the First Amendment was originally written to keep all sects of Christianity on equal footing. Justice Story, an associate justice of the supreme Court wrote in in 1833, *"The real object of the First Amendment was not to countenance, much less to advance, Mahometanism (Islam), or Judaism, or infidelity; by prostrating Christianity; but to exclude all rivalry among Christian sects."*[15] Justice Story also wrote, *"Probably at the time of the adoption of the Constitution, and of the Amendment to it now under consideration, the general, if not the universal, sentiment in America was that Christianity ought to receive encouragement from the State… An attempt to measure all religions and to make it a matter of state policy to hold all in utter indifference would have*

---

created universal disapprobation if not universal indignation. "[16] Justice Story is telling us that that there would have been severe quells in the community had government been erected to stifle Christianity. Today's liberals will claim that the First Amendment is outdated because there are so many other religions in the United States today. However, many of our founders recognized that there were Buddhists, Jews and Muslims residing in America at that time. One of the signers of the Declaration, Benjamin Rush, stated, "such is my veneration for every religion that reveals the attributes of the Deity, or a future state of rewards and punishments, that I had rather see the opinions of Confucius or Mohamed inculcated upon our youth than see them grow up wholly devoid of a system of religious principles. But the religion I mean to recommend in this place is that of the New Testament... All its doctrines and precepts are calculated to promote the happiness of society and the safety of wellbeing of civil government."[17] It appears as long as a religion taught that there was a creator and that that creator offered rewards for good behavior or punishments for bad behavior, that said religion was a good thing. Many of the founders did profess a strong preference of Christianity though, and made that apparent in their state legislations and daily writings.

---

[16] Joseph Story, *A Familiar Exposition of the Constitution of the United States* (New York: Harper & Brothers, 1854), p. 259-261
[17] Benjamin Rush, *Essays, Literary, Moral and Philosophical* (Philadelphia: Thomas & Samuel F. Bradford, 1798) , p. 8, "Of the Mode of Education Proper in a Republic"

Back in the days of the late 1700s, early 1800s there was a great debate among the colonists. It was common knowledge that a people who were governed by themselves, instead of a tyrannical king, would have to be a virtuous society. Benjamin Franklin accurately stated *"Only a virtuous people are capable of freedom. As nations become more corrupt and vicious, they have more need of masters."[18]* If we wonder why Obama got elected, if we wonder why government strangles the innovation of entrepreneurs, if we wonder why we have riots in our streets and religious attacks on Christians, it is because we have become more corrupt and vicious towards one another.

Before we dive into how corrupt and vicious our nation is, just so we as Christians can sit back and think, "Oh at least we're not like them", let me reiterate that the sin of inactivity places blame on us, far more than the vicious and the corrupt. The Bible says in Exodus 18:21 *"Moreover, thou shalt provide out of all the people able men, such as fear God, men of truth, hating covetousness, and place rulers of thousands, rulers of hundreds, rulers of fifties and rulers of tens."* So, we hear the commands of God, who set the foundation for our type of government. People think that God has no references towards political involvement, but the Bible is riddled with guidelines for how government is to be implemented. In this verse, God

---

[18] Taylor, E. (2017). *Only a Virtuous People are Capable of Freedom - National Center for Constitutional Studies*. [online] National Center for Constitutional Studies. Available at: https://nccs.net/2015-03-only-a-virtuous-people-are-capable-of-freedom [Accessed 30 Dec. 2017].

commands that we elect virtuous men to office. That doesn't stop at showing up to a voting booth every two years. It goes much farther beyond that. Political action and volunteering is needed. If you're tired of choosing between the lesser of two evils then go out, get involved and discover virtuous men to run for office, push them to run and then go campaign for them! Every "lesser of two evils" candidate that was nominated was done so through activism! If Christians don't like who those people are, we need to get smart and do exactly what God told us to do. Elect virtuous men to office. This was the Christian way at the birth of our nation.

Chapter 3

"America is great because she is good…"

French jurist Alex De Toqueville was welcomed to our shores in 1831. France, like the rest of the world was wondering, what in the world are those Americans doing? There was an economic explosion coming from the west, eclipsing all the wealth of the European nations combined, but these colonists, just 30 years ago, were a bunch of farmers, blacksmiths and merchants fighting the most powerful military force in the world. How is this happening? They sent Alex De Toqueville across the Atlantic to find out, and found out, he did.

Alex wrote of the nation's heavy overtones of Christianity in his book, Democracy in America. He wrote, *"On my arrival in the United States the religious aspect of the country was the first thing that struck my attention;*

and the longer I stayed there, the more I perceived the great political consequences resulting from the new state of things. "[19] I like to imagine De Toqueville stepping off his ship, breathing in the air of America and being able tell that the atmosphere of this new country was different, virtuous, prosperous. It's hard to imagine just how "new" the idea of self-governance and liberty was. No one had tried this system for thousands of years. Mankind had been ruled for centuries by kings and monarchies that only sought wealth through confiscation and conquest. Now, we see a country that wants to pioneer this new radical idea that produces wealth through commerce, not conquest.

He went on to write, *"In France, I had almost always seen the spirit of religion and the spirit of freedom marching in opposite directions. But in America they were intimately united."*[20] As modern-day Jesus followers, we wonder why freedom and religion would ever march in opposite directions. This sounds very basic to us, that religion and freedom have always walked hand in hand. However, the answer lies deeper in the context of the times. In France, the church was the government, so the church made laws, and proclaimed that you might be a dirty sinner for going against the church. It would be like tea party patriots being called immoral, sinful, idolaters

[19]Teachushistory.org. (2017). *Overview | Teach US History.* [online] Available at: http://www.teachushistory.org/detocqueville-visit-united-states/overview [Accessed 30 Dec. 2017].

[20] Teachushistory.org. (2017). *Overview | Teach US History.* [online] Available at: http://www.teachushistory.org/detocqueville-visit-united-states/overview [Accessed 30 Dec. 2017].

because we believed in less government. In France, we would be believing in less church.

Alex put it extremely well, *"The Revolutionists of America are obliged to profess an ostensible respect for Christian morality and equity, which does not permit them to violate wantonly the laws that oppose their designs...Thus, while the law permits the Americans to do what they please, religion prevents them from conceiving, and forbids them to commit, what is rash or unjust."*[21] This hearkens back to Benjamin Franklin's quote considering a corrupt and vicious nation. Americans didn't need a king to tell them not to shortchange each other. The Bible told them not to. Americans didn't need a heavy-handed ruler to punish theft. The Bible told them not to. Americans didn't need higher earthly authorities to convince them not to commit murder. The Bible told them not to. Americans listened to God, and America prospered.

Alex also spoke of the education in America and the knowledge of the average citizen. *"In New England (the colonies) every citizen receives the elementary notions of human knowledge; he is taught, moreover, the doctrines and the evidences of his religion, the history of his country, and the leading features of his Constitution. In the States of Connecticut and Massachusetts, it is extremely rare to find a man imperfectly acquainted with all these things, and a person wholly ignorant of them is a sort of phenomenon."[22]* I think it would be safe to say that now it is a phenomenon to find someone articulate in history, the Constitution and their religion. Even among the information age with telephones and computers it's obvious that the colonists were even better informed than the population is today. Once again, we are in more need of masters. As viciousness and corruption take a foothold in society, earthly authorities will step in to "right the wrong". If Christians become ignorant of the founder's beliefs and why they believed them, our defense of Biblical government will fall far short from the mark.

Alex goes on to detail how public funds from the Federal government were spent to evangelize the lost. *"The Americans combine the notions of Christianity and of liberty so intimately in their minds that it is impossible to make them conceive the one without the other... I have known of societies formed by Americans to send out ministers of the gospel into the new Western states, to found schools and churches there, lest religion should be allowed to die away in those remote settlements, and the rising states be less fitted to enjoy free institutions than the people from whom they came."[23]*

I've had a few liberal scholars point out to me that Thomas Jefferson was an agnostic who did not believe in

[22] Teachushistory.org. (2017). *Overview | Teach US History*. [online] Available at: http://www.teachushistory.org/detocqueville-visit-united-states/overview [Accessed 30 Dec. 2017].

[23] Teachushistory.org. (2017). *Overview | Teach US History*. [online] Available at: http://www.teachushistory.org/detocqueville-visit-united-states/overview [Accessed 30 Dec. 2017].

the miracles of Jesus. They proclaim that Jefferson tore out the pages of the Bible containing any reference to Jesus' wonderous works because he did not believe Jesus was the Son of God. From this, we get Jefferson's Bible. What these leftists will not tell you is what he did with the pages he tore out. Jefferson believed so fervently that the gospel needed to be shared with the natives that he compiled all of God's miracles into a single, easy to read collection to be dispersed to Native Americans on the frontier. Jefferson, understanding that the Bible could be a challenging study for those just learning how to read, wanted the miracles of the Bible to be shared most among the tribes. That doesn't sound like an agnostic act to me. It sounds more like Jefferson was a dedicated Christian.

Alex wrapped up the entirety of his argument in one simple quote, a quote that I believe stands as the immutable law of our land concerning Christian morality, *"I sought for the greatness and genius of America in her ample rivers, and it was not there; in her fertile fields and boundless prairies and it was not there; in her rich mines and her vast world commerce and it was not there. Not until I went to the churches of America and heard her pulpits aflame with righteousness did I understand the secret of her genius and power. America is great because she is good, and if America ceases to be good, America will cease to be great."*[24]

---

[24] Teachushistory.org. (2017). *Overview | Teach US History.* [online] Available at: http://www.teachushistory.org/detocqueville-visit-united-states/overview [Accessed 30 Dec. 2017].

An Appeal To Heaven

If it's not already obvious, when Christians vacate an area of calling, whatever arena they are stepping out of will leave a vacuum for the corrupt, the power hungry and the self-serving to step in. I think it's apparent that no political figure, whether it be Donald Trump, Hillary Clinton, Ted Cruz or Bernie Sanders, will ever make America great again. This task lies squarely on the shoulders of the church. This is our ordainment to set this right.

When America was first taking steps in rebellion against the crown, the question was raised, where are we going to get our navy? see below - capitalize navy or not for consistency? There were no ships, funds or military. But one man decided to engage himself for the good of his country. George Washington commissioned the first seven vessels of the Continental war fleet out of his own pocket. Keep this in mind, America did not even have a flag to fly over her navy so Washington instructed an "Appeal To Heaven" flag be flown over his vessels. Now the story behind this flag is very intriguing. It is a flag with a white background, a pine tree in the middle and the words "Appeal To Heaven" written boldly across the top. This design was soon adopted by the Massachusetts navy, matched with white and green uniforms and eventually absorbed into the later established, US Navy. Washington not only sacrificed his own money, livelihood and time but he proclaimed clear and loud that the brewing Revolution was to no longer be decided by a king or bureaucracy but delivered up as a last resort; "an appeal to heaven". When the courts fail, when leaders crumble, when the laws of man prove ineffective to keep society in check, this is the last, and most concrete resort we have: an appeal to heaven.

Now the obvious question, "Why the pine tree?" The ancient Iroquois Indians have long held the pine tree in great regards as the tree of peace. Legend had it that a great Native American peacemaker brought 6 warring tribes together to the Great Lakes and united them. As a symbol of their peace, the tribes buried their weapons at the foot of a pine tree. At the top of this tree there was to be a bald eagle clutching 6 arrows (for the six tribes) as a guardian of peace. Any of this sounding familiar yet? Of course, our eagle is clutching 13 arrows symbolizing the 13 original colonies, which once again illustrates how attentive our founders were to history as well. Also, this is where we get the term "bury the hatchet". History isn't so boring after all, is it?

<u>America's First Bible</u>

The very first Bible that was printed in the United States was printed in 1782, and can you guess who printed that Bible? The U.S. Congress. The book was printed using Federal funds, and what's even more intriguing is what it says in the first pages, "A neat edition of the Holy Scriptures for our schools..." It goes on to say, "Congress has resolved that we recommend this edition of the Bible to the inhabitants of the United States." So we see the first Bible ever printed English in the U.S. was done so by the federal government and then recommended to be read in public schools, but yet the modern interpretation of "separation of church and state" trumps all original intent. I hope we can see how the understanding of separation of church and state is very important when we go to defend our positions.

<u>Government Calling Upon the Aid of Religion</u>

As further proof of our founder's loyalty to religion and morality, an oath was administered in court houses across the land, not to hold the oath giver legally accountable, but spiritually accountable. Today, if you are summoned to court you swear an oath to "tell the truth, the whole truth and nothing but the truth so help you God." This practice is used to put in place a procedure to charge the subject with purgery if they lie. The founders looked at the administration of the oath in a slightly different light.

A definition of an oath per 1788 was, "a solemn appeal to the Supreme Being for the truth of what is said by a person who believes in the existence of a Supreme Being and in a future state of rewards and punishments according to that form which would bind his conscious most." Basically, if you were lying in court, the court system figured that any punishment they could levy would not be anywhere near as bad as what God could punish you with should you lie after swearing on His holy word.

Chancellor James Kent (a father of American Jurisprudence) noted that an oath of office was a *"religious solemnity"* and that to administer an oath was *"to call in the aid of religion."* Signer of the Constitution, Rufus King, also noted "[In our*] laws… by the oath which they prescribe, we appeal to the Supreme Being so to deal with us hereafter as we observe the obligation of our oaths. The Pagan world were and are without the mighty influence of this principle which is proclaimed in the Christian system-Their morals were destitute of its powerful sanction while their oaths neither awakened the hopes nor fears which a belief in Christianity inspires."*

The society believed so fervently in this idea that on more than one occasion, court cases would be thrown out if either the defendant or plaintiff did not believe in God. Alex De Tocqueville wrote in his book, *"While I was in America, a witness who happened to be called at the Sessions of the county of Chester(state of New York) declared that he did not believe in the existence of a God or in the immortality of the soul. The judge refused to admit the evidence, on the ground that the witness had destroyed beforehand all the confidence of the court in what he was about to say… the New York spectator of August 23, 1831, related that fact in the following terms: … 'The presiding judge remarked that he had not before been aware that there was a man living who did not believe in the existence of God; that this belief constituted the sanction of all testimony in a court of justice; and that he knew of no case in a Christian country where a witness had been permitted to testify without such belief."*

Why are so many of these evidences glossed over in today's history books? Why are our children not taught these basic ideals in schools? A better question is, why have we not been taught these things? There's much more evidence in the following chapters of encounters and tales of miraculous Providential influence that turned the tides in America's favor, every time. Here's where it really gets interesting.

Chapter 4
That Divine Hand
of Providence

Some of the most compelling evidence of our morality-based society is flippantly glossed over in today's history books. In a number of instances when our country's existence hung on by a thread, fortune always seemed to fall in America's direction no matter how unlikely. Today's history classes teach "history" but unfortunately modern history is mostly memorization of dates, battles, names and places. Obviously, many of today's youth (and adults) find it to be boring and who could blame them? If we can teach "history with a purpose" instead of preparing for next week's exam, then maybe we can return our culture to one that reveres the teachings of yesteryear. Until then… You'll just have to read this book!

There are many various lessons we can glean from the early days of colonization in America. Numerous attempts had been made to establish settlements in the New World, years before the Pilgrims boarded the Mayflower. If we look at an attempt by renowned atheist, Sir Walter Raleigh, we can see God's hand of protection didn't seem to shield the ambitions of this excursion. During the 1580's Raleigh attempted three separate times to colonize Roanoke Island off the shores of modern day North Carolina. The first group was in such misery that they took the first chance they could with a passing ship headed back to England. The last attempt that was made resulted in a mystery that goes unsolved to this day: "the Lost Colony". Governor John White, leader of the colony, pledged to return within a year with badly needed supplies and food for his settlement and returned to England. The situation was dire for the inhabitants of Roanoke but many stayed, deciding to brave the elements and the savages. To White's behest, his ship was severely slowed thanks to several stops by the Spanish Armada and complications from England's war with Spain. John's travels were delayed by nearly 3 years.

He returned on August 18th, 1590 to find that his family, friends and workers had completely vanished. For years, historians and archeologists have tried to explain the incident with little success. The camps had been left, undisturbed, with no sign of a struggle or any kind of attack. The only clues that could be found were the letters "CRO" chiseled into a post and the word "Croatoan" carved into a tree trunk. The nearby island of "Croatoan" seemed to be the first place to investigate but the search turned up nothing. Modern archeologists have found just a few fragments of 16th century pottery on the island but very little to suggest an entire settlement had once lived there. Reports from the local hostile tribes claimed responsibility for the disappearance but conflicting stories would never line up chronologically. Some rumors persisted that "white Indians" had been seen some generations later, compelling some to believe that the tribe at Roanoke simply assimilated in with the local Indian villages and mated with them. Numerous other rumors float around to this day but it's doubtful anyone will ever know the true happenings on Roanoke island over 4 centuries ago.

The next attempt to colonize the Americas was Jamestown in 1607. This particular expedition exerted a more religious tone as its purpose for colonization. James I commissioned the expedition with the asking of "the Providence of Almighty God" to assist them in the "propagating of Christian Religion to such people, as yet live in darkness and miserable ignorance." In other words, the colonists wished to evangelize the natives. Even though this worthy cause sought protection from God it did not necessarily guarantee success or safety.

The colonists donned a system of socialism to govern themselves which led to disaster. The inhabitants of Jamestown had fallen into the trap of a society for the common good. No one individual had rights to any land and the farming was all done as a community service. At the community food bank, people could drop off several bushels of corn while picking up some fresh meat someone else had killed but this, of course, did not transpire as planned. As could be expected, someone could come to the storehouse and drop off a head of lettuce but take several baskets of corn, some meat, and maybe some grain without any accountability or oversight. It was easy for people to abuse the system, and so individuals would often take advantage of "the common good" by not working and allowing others to take on the burden of feeding the colony. Once colonists figured out that they really didn't have to work, they didn't! As the pantries went bare and the food rations plummeted, the colonists started blaming each other for not pulling their own weight. This dire situation worsened and before 1607 had ended; 66 of 104 colonists had died from starvation or sickness. After the first 6 months of 1609, 440 of 500 that had recently arrived, also died. Things in Jamestown took a very dark turn for the worst when rescuers from England showed up to find colonists turning on each other and resulting to cannibalism for food. Socialism always looks good on paper and in theory, but Capitalism is what steps in and demands individual responsibility.

Sir Thomas Dale saw the barbaric results of a socialistic society and made plans to return the colony back to humanity. It took 4 years to turn the situation around but Dale reinstated property rights, giving each colonist over an acre of land and giving them responsibility over it for their own survival. The community storehouse was abolished, and individual responsibility reinstated. Once colonists started producing again, it was possible for them to start trading with one another and selling wares, food and goods, leading to prosperity and blessings. Once again, Capitalism, a system ordained by the Holy Scriptures in I Thessalonians 3:10, was the answer to the colonists' problems and remains the most effective, poverty busting system the world has ever seen to this day.

This leads us to the tale of the Pilgrims. This story has been redundantly told thousands of times in elementary schools across the country, but few know the actual miraculous path that this band of Jesus followers embarked on over 300 years ago.

Contrary to popular belief the Pilgrims, also derided by the term "Puritans" from those who looked down upon them, embarked on their journey not from England but from Holland. The Puritans had originally sought to rid themselves from the Church of England, a church, they believed, to be driven more by men and their own desires rather than God and His Will. The group of a few more than a thousand people were disregarded as a radical, dangerous and illegal group of extremists wanting to take over the church. The Pilgrims simply wanted to worship in a way that wasn't administered by man but how they felt would be pleasing to God.

After fleeing England, the band of Christians settled into Holland, a very religiously tolerant nation. After several years in Holland, they began to worry that the influence of the Church of England, as well as materialism and bustling commerce would have a negative impact on their children. Amid these concerns, they began to lobby investors for funds to travel to the new world and begin life anew. As private investors signed onto the idea, the pioneers of a new Christian society made plans to cross the Atlantic in a little over 30 days. The Pilgrims had been given permission to land in what would now be New York. The island of Manhattan was designated for their colonization as it was known for receiving the occasional merchant or company of fisherman and could help keep the colony fed.

Life aboard the ship did not go as planned. The ocean was wrought with rough seas and storms. Navigational problems haunted the trip and the living conditions on board deteriorated rapidly as the trip extended far past the original time frame, lasting a long 66 days. By the time the Pilgrims saw land they realized they had missed their landing by over 250 miles, a possible deadly miscalculation. Upon seeing the shoreline, their leader, William Bradford recalled, "Being thus arrived in a good harbor and brought safe to land, they fell upon their knees and blessed the God of Heaven, who had brought them over the vast and furious ocean, and delivered them from all the perils and miseries thereof, again to set their feet on stable earth, their proper element." The mood seemed to be consistent among the men, including Bradford, that with no welcoming parties, stores, places to rest or luxuries and with their back to an unending sea, the only solace the young pioneers could take would be none other than God Almighty. Despite the setbacks from the trip, the pilgrims confided in their God and banded together into what was the first legal Constitution of the New World, the Mayflower Compact which read,

"Having undertaken for the Glory of God and advancement of the Christian Faith and Honour of our King and Country, a Voyage to plant the First Colony in the Northern Parts of Virginia, do by these presents solemnly and mutually in the presence of God and one of another, Covenant and Combine ourselves together in a Civil Body Politic, for our better ordering and preservation and furtherance of the ends aforesaid; and by virtue hereof to enact, constitute and frame such just and equal Laws, Ordinances, Acts, Constitutions and Offices from time to time, as shall be thought most meet and convenient for the general good of the Colony, unto which we promise all due submission and obedience."

The compact was signed on November 11th, 1620 upon the landing of Cape Cod for the expressed purpose of spreading the gospel of Jesus Christ.

The group decided to move the ship and try to navigate their way back down the coastline to Manhattan in hopes of survival but attempt after attempt proved useless as the November winds repeatedly pushed their ship back to the same location they had landed. Many, feeling that this was some way of God's Providence directing them to stay in Plymouth, decided to set up camp there and start making provisions for colonization.

The early days were fraught with bitter cold and the constant threat of wolves, or worse yet, the savage natives. As exploration of the surrounding areas began, the colonists discovered a vast Indian camp, formerly known as Patuxet, completely deserted and devoid of life. The local maps had mentioned a stash of corn in the area which would give them much needed food for the rest of the winter. The pilgrims began searching for the rightful owners of the corn, fearing that their taking would be theft, but no others could be found. The people banded together a pact stating that the corn would be paid back in any way possible should the rightful owners turn up, but thankfully the pilgrims had been blessed with a decent stash of food to assist them in the remaining cold months ahead. "And sure, it was God's good providence that we found this corn for else we know not how we should have done.", remarked Edward Winslow. Luckily the Indians had cleared the area of brush and trees making the place an ideal camp for their settlement, lacking any good avenues from stealthy attacks from local natives.

Even though the Pilgrims praised God for their good fortune, their experience did not go without serious strife and death. As winter drew down to a close, the cost of life was a sharp sting to the lives of the colonists. Forty-seven of the 102 settlers had starved, frozen or died of illnesses. However, their luck was about to take another turn in a positive direction.

On March 16, 1621 a strange native revealed himself to the colony. Introducing himself as Samoset, they were surprised to hear that the native could string together words of broken English in attempting to communicate with them. The man stayed with them, at the settler's discomfort, the entire night, speaking as an excited schoolboy would about his story. He had befriended fisherman from England and had ferried a ship from further south to bring him there. He went on to explain that the Indian settlement they had found had been ravaged by a merciless plague. Not one survivor had made it through the sickness, wiping out the entire tribe.

Modern day historians and archeologists claim that the shorelines of Plymouth had been heavily populated with native tribes right up until the time the Pilgrims arrived. Horrid illnesses, probably spread by infected food from local fisherman and tradesman had wiped out entire colonies of natives making the area peculiarly safe just in time for the Puritans from England to land ashore. Many of the pilgrims rejoiced in the timing of God's plan, never once thinking negatively of the Indians but with respect to the loss of life for their sake. Had these certain diseases not manifested themselves at the precise time that they did, colonization and survival would have been impossible for the zealous group of Christians.

A few days after Samoset's departure, he returned with another native in tow, this native having a remarkably fluent comprehension of not only the English language but English customs and religion as well. He introduced himself as Tisquantum, or "Squanto" as the white man had called him. The settlers soon found out that he was the last sole survivor of the tribe that had lived at Patuxet. The only method of his survival? Being kidnapped into slavery at the age of twelve by an English fisherman in 1605. The fisherman had brought him back to England to show off as a trophy and local wonder as the "tribesman from the New World". After 9 long years of being homesick, Squanto managed to escape and received passage back to the new world on a ship captained by John Smith, a leader of the Jamestown colony. Squanto had made it so close to returning home after the voyage, even seeing the shoreline to his home of Patuxet, but he once again found himself kidnapped by one of Captain Smith's less ethical business partners. The young native was forced into the hold of another ship alongside 20 other native captives and was shipped all the way back to Spain in a cramped, wet and unsanitary compartment in the belly of the carrier. Once arriving in Spain, Squanto was sold to the Spanish church. The monks were ardently against enslavement of the natives of America and decided to buy them out of captivity. The monks and clergymen brought Squanto back to full health, taught him about the gospel of Jesus Christ and upon Squanto's request, sent him back to England to live with a Christian family who sharpened his English skills. After several years with the family he was able to secure passage back to the New World and was finally on his way home.

Upon arriving, Squanto returned to his village to find not a soul stirring. Panicked, he went to the other surrounding tribes looking for answers. They relayed the news to him of the passing of his tribe and the horrid disease that had taken them. Squanto lived for a few months by himself before assimilating with the Wampanoag tribe, the dominate tribe of the region and soon after met with the pilgrims.

The pilgrims, astonished at their good fortune to find an English-speaking Indian, invited Squanto to stay with them. In the months to come, Squanto served as the mediator between the Indian chief of the Wampanoags and the new settlers. A peace agreement was reached, and the two communities lived in harmony with each other. Squanto also instructed the pilgrims how to properly plant corn and other crops, a practice which undoubtedly saved them from starvation during the upcoming winter. The mediator also instilled a belief in surrounding Indian tribes that the survival of the Pilgrims was a directive from God and their protection and prosperity was Divinely inspired. The peace treaty that was secured lasted over 50 years as the Pilgrims and Indians flourished together in a great time of harmony. Thanks to Squanto and the intricately woven surrounding circumstances, the Pilgrims succeeded in their quest for a new colony. In 1622 Squanto made a journey with several tribe leaders to renew their agreement but fell ill on the journey back. He resolved to travel back to the settlers and according to writings from William Bradford, Squanto made a public declaration of faith, claiming Christ as his savior before slipping into eternity.

The circumstances surrounding the survival of the Pilgrims seems so highly unlikely that any soul should find the happenings as influence of the Divine Providence.

After having sailed 250 miles off course, finding a once populated land now devoid of dangerous savages, a stash of food to last them their first winter, and then finding what was probably the only English-speaking native on the entire continent willing to broker peace among the two groups is simply astonishing and nothing short of a miracle. And this isn't the only instance of Divine intervention on our behalf.

Chapter 5
The Untouchable Washington

Throughout Washington's life, many of his associates and friends would marvel at his obvious ability to cheat death on a multitude of occasions. Washington, by the age of 17 was already an accomplished surveyor, drawing maps and diagrams of the frontier. Living a life past one's teen years was an accomplishment but to also provide for oneself and brave the dangers of the frontier was an even more notable endeavor.

In July 1752, the then 20-year-old Washington mourned the loss of his brother, James, and subsequently took responsibility of his position leading the Virginia militia. Not long after, the Lieutenant Governor of Virginia assigned Washington with a task to deliver an ultimatum to a French outpost on the outskirts of American territories.

France had just begun staking claim to lands on the border of English property and had to be reminded that their actions were not going unnoticed by the King of England. These actions eventually lead to the French Indian War, sometimes known as the Seven Years War, in which Washington also repeatedly escaped bodily harm.

Washington set out to endure 500 miles of wilderness travel into what is now modern-day Pennsylvania. Upon delivering the letter, the leader of the French garrison responded with a stubborn reply that France had rights to the land that they were now occupying. The young militiaman, eager to return the letter back to Virginia ignored all the warnings of dangerous winter travel and decided to embark on a return journey just 10 days before Christmas.

Washington could hear the past warnings repeating from the harsh elements whispering through the pines, but after several days into the trip it was too late to heed them now. Washington and his fellow frontiersman guide, Christopher Gist, ran across a seemingly friendly native who promised to help show them the way to more hospitable territory. After some miles of traveling, the Indian guide offered to carry the trio's heavy muskets. Gist, untrustingly handed over the firearms, insistent on keeping a close eye on the guide. As the three men began walking into a bright clear field the native struck off running about 15 paces before turning around, aiming directly at Washington and firing. For a fraction of a second, as the musket shot pierced through the air, all of eternity held its breath as the fate of a future revolutionary experiment hung perilously in the balance. The fate of the way of living for the entire world depended on where that musket ball landed. Should the future revolutionary war General and president be struck down now, all hope would have been lost for the future colonists. The great idea of American self-governance would never be born. Miraculously the Indian warrior missed by mere inches, his shot landing with a crack inside the trunk of a nearby tree. Gist and Washington both advanced on the traitor beating him and removing him of all weapons. A bloodied Indian limped back into the forest a wiser man, and back to his tribe, more empty handed than when he had left.

The remainder of the trip proved equally perilous as water crossings nearly drowned the two of them. A makeshift raft proved alarmingly unreliable and, upon being splintered by enormous chunks of ice, it left the duo to swim to a mid-stream island. This left Washington to sleep all night in ice hardened clothing. The bitter night was so cold they woke up the next morning to see the river had completely frozen over, allowing passage. How hyperthermia did not set in and freeze them both to death is a mystery.

The stories that permeated the press of Washington's return bolstered the young adventurer into higher military ranks where he led men into battle numerous times at the young age of 23. Washington remarked on the exhilaration of battle, "I heard the bullets whistle, and believe me, there is something charming in the sound." Obviously, being close enough to hear musket shot whistle past shows just how mired in the battle Washington would sometimes be. Reports all throughout Washington's life from men he fought beside exclaimed the near recklessness the General exuded in the heat of battle. From centering himself in a flurry of French gunfire or commanding troops in the rain of British mortar fire, Washington's bravery in the face of danger was not only astonishing but miraculous.

As tensions rose between the French and British over the disagreements over frontier property rights, Washington decided to assist the British during the French Indian War. His mother protested fervently his involvement in military affairs. He responded, "The God to whom you commended me, madam, when I set out upon a more perilous errand, defended me from all harm, and I trust He will do so now. Do not you?" She eventually relented, "With His blessing you can be a useful man in war as in peace, and without it you can expect nothing."

With this, Washington set off to assist the British in navigating the wilds of the frontier. Before long, the French Indian War was being fought across the globe, but more importantly, in Washington's own backyard. The young navigator was assigned to support General Edward Braddock in a mission to take Fort Dusquesne alongside the Monongahela River. Washington had already been suffering from an awful bout of what colonists called "the bloody flux" and had to make much of the trip in a wagon. As the 1500 British regulars marched within a few miles of the French occupied fort, Washington resolved to ride in the saddle again, strongly cautioning General Braddock away from using traditional British military methods of meeting their enemies on an open field. Washington knew of the dangers and tactics the Indian populations west of the colonies, but Braddock resolved to keep his soldiers marching in traditional lines through the woods, ripe for the picking during any attempted ambush. As Englishmen, it was considered proper warfare to meet your opponents on the field, firing, reloading and firing again in perfect formation. Braddock, even vastly outnumbering his opponent by nearly 600 men, was not prepared for the carnage that would ensue by ignoring Washington's warnings.

The morning of July 9th, 1755, shots rang out all through the trees as Edward Braddock moved his troops in closer. Lines of redcoats tumbled to the ground in pain, agony and blood as the smoke clouds plumed from French muskets in the woods. As the shots kept raining down upon his men, seemingly from nowhere, the horses panicked, sensing the fear and confusion of the British regulars. The natives weaved in and out of the trees, as silent spirits or thick mists would, never firing in volleys but with a constant randomness that kept the British from being able to recompose their forces. The men wasted precious ammunition into the trunks of trees, firing where their attackers had been, mere moments before. Many panicked regulars began sprinting for the back of their regiments and anywhere they could find cover from the hail of musket shot. Washington, seeing the pandemonium, began spurring his horse from the rear of the battalion, desperately attempting to rout the obvious chaos that had gripped his men.

He arrived at the front lines, shouting orders and attempting to bring his men into some kind of formation. As he drew his cutlass, and began circling his troops, a thud pierced the chaos of the battle and rippled through his horse sending her crashing down into the dirt and blood. Luckily the landing did not pin Washington or break his legs upon impact, leaving him to continue fighting on the ground. He was eventually able to retrieve another horse from a fellow fallen officer. As hours passed in the battle, bodies began littering the forest floor. The violence of the scenario made it increasingly hard for his steed to walk without trampling the bodies of the fallen. The smell of death and gun powder mixed rife in the air, making his horse anxious as he rode back and forth rallying his troops. As British regulars began to form behind Washington, the Indian chiefs gave orders to take down any and all mounted officers. "Make sure he dies!" As the armies exchanged gunfire and escalated the fight further, Washington noticed several tugs at his jacket but he kept spurring his horse into enemy fire, slashing any Frenchman or Indian that would dare get close. Gritting his teeth, he felt once again the thud of a musket ball tearing into his horse and her legs collapsing underneath her. Another horse shot from under him, Washington sprang back up and continued fighting.

Washington was soon made aware of the now dying Braddock and had to carry out Braddock's orders as General. Edward Braddock had been wounded in the arm, with a musket ball lying hotly lodged into his lung. "We will know better how to deal with them another time" he told Washington before sending him back to the battle to carry out Braddock's last orders. The evening brought an end to the battle with 977 British Regulars being killed or wounded from a full force that started out as 1,459. Too many of the British had returned fire on their own men amid the confusion, adding to the list of the dead. Every single officer had been shot from their saddle, except for the one, George Washington.

Later that night at the campfire as Washington removed his officer's cloak to warm himself by the fire, a private militia man directed his attention back to his jacket. "What's that sir?" Washington, astonished at his fortitude, surveyed the 4 musket shot holes in his jacket. Shots that had missed his chest and torso by mere inches. "There's another one in your hat sir.", the militia man pointed out. Sure enough, upon the inspection of his hat a musket ball had gone right through. Washington shook his head in disbelief as he ran his finger through the hole trying to comprehend the Divine intervention that had saved his life that day. He later wrote back to his family, *"By the miraculous care of Providence, I have been protected against all human probability or expectation… For I had 4 bullets in my coat and 2 horses shot under me, yet escaped unhurt… Although death was leveling my companions on every side of me."*

Years later, during Washington's encampment at Valley Forge, an Indian chief named Redhawk requested to meet with the commander. The troops cautiously brought the Indian chief into Washington's tent, watching his every move. The chief cleared his throat and began, "*I have traveled a long and weary path that I might see the young warrior of the great battle. It was on the day when the white man's blood mixed with the streams of our forest when I first beheld you. I called to my young men and said 'Quick! Let your aim be certain! He dies!' Our rifles were leveled, rifles which but for you, knew not how to miss. Twas all in vain. A power far mightier than we shielded you. Seeing you were under the special guardianship of the great spirit we immediately ceased to fire at you. I have come to pay homage to the man who is the particular favorite of heaven and who can never die in battle. I am old, and soon shall be gathered to the great council-fire of my fathers, in the land of shades, but ere I go, there is something bids me speak, in the voice of prophecy. Listen! The Great Spirit protects that man, and guides his destinies – He will become the chief of nations, and a people yet unborn, will hail him as the founder of a mighty empire!*"

On September 8th, 1779 the Revolutionary war was raging. General Washington and another field operations officer departed their camp to survey the surrounding areas for reconnaissance. The two officers made their way to a clearing, coming within sight of four British sharpshooters stationed in the trees. Major Patrick Ferguson was the leader of the group and was a renowned marksman.

Ferguson was famous for his invention of the "Ferguson rifles" that were introduced to the British snipers and hailed for their deadly accuracy that rivaled any other gun of the day. Ferguson and his men stiffened at the chance to take down two Continental officers but upon sighting them in, Ferguson felt an odd injustice in shooting a man unprepared. He noted that the officer carried himself quite well upon his steed. Several moments went by as Washington's body was firmly inside Ferguson's crosshairs, but the Major kept arguing with himself on the nobility of shooting such a man. Ferguson blinked and the General rode back out of sight. He later declared, "I could have lodged half a dozen balls in him before he was out of my reach, but it was not pleasant to fire at the back of an unoffending individual who was acquitting himself of his duty – So I let him live… I am sorry that I did not know at the time who it was."

To not see the intervention of God's hand in Washington's life would be a disregard of factual history. Washington, a Godly man who cheated death that day under the scope of Ferguson's rifle, remained resilient against hypothermia in the wilds of Pennsylvania, the only remaining officer left standing on the battlefield beside the Monongahela River, had two horses shot from underneath him, four bullet holes through his uniform and another through his hat would go on to lead the Continental Army to victory in the Revolutionary War, forever changing the course of world history, religious freedoms and free markets for decades and centuries to come.

Chapter 6
Revolutionary Timing

Washington surveyed the rolling plains of New York through his spy glass, planning his next move. Neither the General, nor his nearby aide, French General Rochambeau, could have ever guessed that these rolling hills would one day be a bustling metropolis of commuters and workers carrying out the American dream from day to day. The situation at hand was much more dire. The lands of New York stood not yet as an example of American ingenuity and Capitalism but as a pitted battleground, still stained with the blood of Washington's earlier defeats during the beginning of the war for independence. Now 6 years later, the General weighed his options heavily. He could feel the war coming to an end. Both sides were bloodied and bruised. Back in England the struggle had grown unpopular and costly. The patience of the English people waned as did the provisions and moral of the

Continental Army. In striking New York, the rebels could cause just enough of a stalemate to begin peace talks but perhaps not a decisive blow that would force British surrender. "New York Harbor," Washington said under his breath. The general beckoned towards his French ally. "Should we strike decisively and quick perhaps we can put an end to this skirmish."

Rochambeau strode along side his commander, taking in the layout of the port town. "Cornwallis has fled the South. He resides in Yorktown. Should we capture his force it should be a most swift and final movement needed for our forces. A siege of sorts could end this war."

Washington lowered his spy glass, inquisitively glancing at the Frenchman. "Yorktown is already heavily fortified. Cornwallis enjoys the luxury of a British navy at his back. What would you have? That we lay siege to the town while Cornwallis relaxes among brothels and his company as the sea resupplies his every need? No, I cannot spare the men to make the march and brave such a risk with no real reward."

The Frenchman had encouraged Washington often enough to turn the troops towards Yorktown that the grizzled veteran began to feel a tinge of annoyance at the suggestion. Listening to the counsel of his advisors was always a strong suit for Washington. Unlike many top-down, heavy handed methods used by European armies, the Continental army utilized much input from lower ranks sometimes resulting in wiser choices. However, it was a known fact that the capture of Yorktown served no purpose as long as Cornwallis utilized his navy to indefinitely supply his troops.

"Sir… What if we had a Navy ourselves?" Washington starred back, cautiously hiding any excitement at the idea. Rochambeau who had been in communication with King Louis XVI, produced a letter from his pocket branded with the royal French seal.

"My good sir," He said, handing over the message, "Comte de Grasse sends word of his departure from the West Indies. He boasts 25 warships… Three thousand men."

Washington quickly rounded his top commanders together to unveil his plan of misinformation and deception, a trait that Washington was skilled at. That evening he directed his officers that the troops camped in the wilderness were not to be alerted as to where they were going. Specific pockets of misguided information would be spread to known British spies. Washington also ordered the French to set up camps and cooking boilers to feed several thousand men and place it on the outskirts of White Plains, not far from prying British eyes. The guise that an impending attack on New York would soon take place, left the British wasting valuable resources to further fortify the city. The general looked towards his officers, "Having been betrayed by loose tongues in the past… Perhaps we can use loose tongues to help us now."

During the marches, soldiers would place bets on which city they were going to fire upon, whether that be

New York or Yorktown. The risk was still high for General Washington. Relying on other men for the whole result of the war was unnerving. Not only would the French fleet have to show up at precisely the right time, a gamble in itself, but Comte de Grasse would have to fend off the superior British Men of War that patrolled the coast and the Chesapeake Bay. However, if this did work, the Continentals could surround Cornwallis and force a victory. The men had been so beaten down these past years with only a few victories to tie them on, a successful siege on a British commander's outpost would surely bring the boys alight with joy!

On September 5th, Cornwallis was startled from his evening dinner as blasts could be heard from across the Chesapeake Bay. British intelligence had intercepted news that a French fleet was on its way, but no one had entertained the idea that it would show up on Cornwallis' back door! In anticipation of an attack on New York, Cornwallis and Admiral Thomas Graves both agreed to send ships to NY harbor, but outrage ran through the commander's blood as he discovered that every ship had been sent north. If the French navy had come to Chesapeake Bay looking for a fight, then that meant that Washington and his men were soon to follow. Letters went out to Admiral Graves admonishing him for recalling the entire fleet to his harbor, but Graves relayed back to Yorktown that many of the British ships that had been recalled were already undergoing repairs and could not immediately be dispatched back to Virginia. Cornwallis pounded his fist on the desk in frustration. If the British fleet did not return soon, Yorktown would be surrounded.

On September 18, 1781, Washington and his troops arrived on the outskirts of the port city, their numbers massively bolstered to 17,000 to faceoff the 9,000 British regulars that lay in wait within the city walls.

French troops, numbering 5,500, had made land fall in nearby Gloucester county and were dispatched to the western front of Yorktown with Washington's Continentals on the east. Cornwallis had a chain of seven redoubts strung around the marshes of the city. Berms of earth fortified with sharpened pine tree trunks and cannon were to be the first target of the arriving patriots. Washington instructed his troops to start digging a massive line of trenches, edging closer and closer to the British lines.

On September 29th Washington's men got close enough to start inviting British cannon fire. Being almost out of range, the casualties were minimal. The general resolved to get right down into the mud and dirt with his men, also lending a hand in the digging process. Everyday, his men drew closer and closer to the city, taking out redoubts as they worked along. Many men marveled at the sheer bravery or ignorance of Washington standing time and time again in the line of fire as cannonade erupted around him. While surveying the trenches a cannonball landed very near to Washington, a deafening thunder of light and noise as it erupted among his officers. Rochambeau had been knocked from his seat and remained blinded and deaf from the explosion for several seconds after. When his sense finally came back he realized he had rolled into one of the nearby trenches, dirt and rocks still raining down against his back and shoulders. As the smoke cleared away, there was General Washington, staring through his spy glass as if no sound, light or explosion had ever occurred. He looked down to his feet where a chaplain's hat lay. Chaplain Evans scrambled up from the ground, astonished at his good fortune. Washington knelt, retrieved the hat, noted the singe marks around the outside brim and handed it back to the chaplain. "Mr. Evans," he smiled, "you had better take that hat home to show your wife and children."

As the trenches grew longer and closer to the city, Continental forces systematically picked off regiments of redcoats stationed at each redoubt. The war outside the city walls proved quite bloody but the Americans seemed to have the upper hand, both in numbers and in spirit.

Time began to pass slowly for the increasingly pressured Cornwallis. Supplies were beginning to wane and General Graves in New York seemed to have no urgency in returning the British fleet to Yorktown as he felt repairs should be thoroughly completed before sailing out. Some action had to be taken. As mid-October began approaching as did the Continental army, Cornwallis made plans to surrender Yorktown, of course, pending his escape. The Chesapeake Bay offered little cover for escape due to a well-lit moon but finally the General timed the night for the moon to disappear and take his chance.

The moonless night of October 13th, the water of the bay was pitch black, as was everything else. Cornwallis loaded some of his finest officers on a boat to make the first crossing to Gloucester county and flee back to New York. The first boat passed over the waters, in complete silence, unmolested by enemy fire or notice. As Cornwallis awaited the return, a massive storm seemed to arise out of nowhere. Sudden winds swept the boats far off course, some capsizing and leaving redcoats fighting to swim back to shore. Lightning flashed, and the seas grew deathly chaotic, almost smashing what was left of the returning boats against the coastline rocks. It seemed as though, within a matter of seconds the calm sea had been ripped apart by violent waves and crashing foam. Cornwallis cursed the sky as his only chance at escape had been foiled. By the next morning Cornwallis had exhausted his ammunition, instilling an eerie quietness to the front lines. The Americans continued shelling the fortifications relentlessly. He would have to face Washington's conditions if Grave's fleet did not show up soon.

October 13th, General Graves began preparing his Navy for departure. The general was almost giddy at the chance to decimate French forces on his preferred battlefield of the sea. That morning however, another conveniently timed storm swept the New York harbor. Strong squalls battered the ships in the bay, severely damaging the masts of two of the lead ships, the *Shrewsbury* and the *Alcide*. This setback would hinder the British fleet for another week, trying once again to repair even more damage. The British Navy was effectively out of commission for the time being, leaving Cornwallis to face the humiliation of surrender. Some historians document these two storms as mere coincidence but if you were to ask any of the patriots they would have told you that the hand of God was moving against their opponent.

Finally, in a painfully shameful last resort, Cornwallis surrendered his 8,000 troops to General George Washington on October 20th, 1781. Embarrassed that the battle-tested British general had been bested by his own former subjects, Cornwallis, in contrast to the normal procedure of displaying defeat, issued his Brigadier General to offer the sword of surrender to General Rochambeau. The Frenchman, realizing the slight Cornwallis was trying to give to Washington by not showing up in person, refused it. He pointed to Washington, considering he had been the chief architect to the plan but Washington also refused to accept the sword from a lower ranking officer. He directed the British Brigadier to one of his deputies, thereby displaying victory for his troops and the hope of the American experiment.

By the time the British fleet arrived, it was too late. Word was sent to New York of Yorktown's surrender, but General Graves had already left after finally getting his fleet in order. The general arrived on October 25th, shocked to see that the French fleet had already docked in Chesapeake Bay. Graves looked on in horror as the force he was made aware of was much larger in strength and number than he had originally anticipated. The French Navy officer, De Grasse, confidently dispatched 24 ships out to meet the 19 British Men of War in an all-out battle to once again reaffirm hostilities between Great Britain and France. The ships of both fleets lined up, exchanged shot after shot. Cannonballs whistled through the air, splinters of hulls and masts sprayed the faces of the crewmen. All out war broke out on the water for over 2 hours. The British took heavy losses with one of the largest ships, the *Terrible*, sustaining fatal damage to her foremast. The ship was ordered to be sunk as crews could not repair the damage quickly enough out of port. The British began distancing themselves from the fleet and started exchanging fire from longer distances, no longer able to face off with the superior French forces. De Grasse chased Graves' men out of the Chesapeake Bay and further away from Yorktown. Eventually the chase broke off and De Grasse returned. Graves, humiliated, limped his fleet back to New York.

As the surrendering ceremonies began, obvious British resentment permeated the formalities. Eight thousand British troops marched between the French and American forces. Many men on both sides openly wept, some for joy, some for utter disgust. As British weapons were handed over some of the Regulars simply threw them to the ground, stomping them and attempting to render them useless. As the 8,000 men marched between the columns of victors the British band keyed a quite appropriate song "The World Turned Upside Down".

Listen to me and you shall hear,

News hath not been this thousand year;

Since Herod, Caesar, and many more,

you never heard the like before.

The redcoats would not face the Americans and would only take notice of the French forces. Rochambeau, noticing the disrespect, keyed up his own band, loudly playing an instantly recognizable American chorus of "Yankee Doodle Dandy". By the time the Americans joined in, the Redcoats could hardly be heard.

Washington had done it. He had won the impossible war. He had "turned the world upside down". As we look at this story we see that the impeccable and unlikely timing of the French fleet, perfectly disguised misinformation and the heavenly assistance of two well timed storms could not have all been simple coincidence. Considering the many stories, several that aren't even mentioned in this book, we can easily see that God had a specific plan for this New World and its people. Once again, as Washington lamented, *"No people can be bound to acknowledge and adore the Invisible Hand which conducts the affairs of men more than those of the United States. Every step by which they have advanced to the character of an independent nation seems to have been distinguished by some token of Providential Agency."* Historian Charles Bracelen Floor discovered in his studies that there were at least sixty-seven pivotal moments during the war where miraculous circumstances turned the winds of favor in Washington's direction, allowing the embers of freedom to glow for just one more battle, one more day.

This is our call to action. God obviously has a plan for the United States, and He has one for you too! He has a plan for your influence if you allow Him to guide it. There is no doubt that the American Revolution was guided by the hand of Providence, much a credit to the people who took action and reaped God's blessings on their land. Now we must fill that role. American independence would not have happened if God's people hadn't moved. The same speaks true today. If we don't put action behind our faith, God's hands and feet cannot move in our society! Take these stories as inspiration and evidence of our involvement in political affairs as we explore in the next chapter the appropriateness of Christian involvement in the State.

Chapter 7
The Separation of
Church and State

Many of us may have come across someone who constantly uses that phrase "separation of church and state". If anyone is practicing their faith anywhere other than at home or church or any private property, according to current laws, the government can shut down whatever public act of religion we may be involved with. We've seen this with nativity scenes. We've seen this with the Ten Commandments in court rooms. We've seen this with prayer in public schools, and the list goes on and on and it all comes down to that phrase, "the separation of church and state." How do we tactfully combat this? First, we must understand its origins. The first thing you can tell your atheist friend is to ask them, "What federal document contains that language?" Of course, it is not contained in any founding document. We had 90 founding fathers and there is no proof at all of any of them uttering or dictating the phrase "separation of church and state" during the founding of our nation. So where did it come from?

On November 7th, 1801 the Danbury Baptist Church wrote a letter to then president, Thomas Jefferson.[25] The church was very concerned about the bill of rights. Looking back today one would wonder, why would a church have a problem with the bill of rights; specifically, the first amendment? Now the first amendment "prohibits the making of any law respecting an establishment of religion, or prohibiting the free exercise thereof..." Today it doesn't make any sense that the church would be worried with this, but we must look at the way of thinking the people had developed back then. During the late 1700s-early 1800s people believed in Natural Law, or in other words, God's Law. Natural Law stated that a person had a right to own property, to pursue wealth, to bear arms, the right to habeas corpus, checks and balances, the list goes on. It was perceived that putting Natural Law in text, in writing, would lower its prestige right alongside the common laws of man. They believed that if Natural Law were written down, one day the government could decide to repeal it, just as any other law of the day. This is how genuine the people's faith and respect for Natural law was. This was how deep the ideas of Natural Law were

---

[25] WallBuilders. (2017). *Letters Between the Danbury Baptists and Thomas Jefferson - WallBuilders*. [online] Available at: https://wallbuilders.com/letters-danbury-baptists-thomas-jefferson/ [Accessed 30 Dec. 2017].

embedded into the fabric of our society. They thought, if everyone already knows these laws, why write them down? The Danbury Baptists believed putting it into the Constitution made it appear to be a right granted by the government and not the Almighty.

Jefferson, fully understanding their intent, wrote back to them, reassuring them that there was a "clear wall of separation between church and state." We see here that this initial phrase from Jefferson was intended to protect the church from the government and not the government from the church. The separation of church and state was intended to be used in an entirely different way during the birth of our nation. Our founders were very religious people, very Christian people and they involved God in everything they did, whether it was privately at home or publicly in the capitol. But they also realized the destruction that a church-run government could have on a nation and people's Natural Inalienable rights. This was done so to prevent another regime of oppressive, authoritative religion run by man, similar to the Church of England. This is where we must understand the intent of the separation phrase.

Even in the Bible God ordained three structures for Christianity to live prosperously in a society. He ordained the family for our immediate relationships. He ordained the civil government for our societal relationships; "whoever sheds man's blood, by him shall man's blood be shed." And then we see the 3rd ordainment, the establishment of the church. We see in Romans 13 that

God did not give the sword to the church, He gave it to the government. God knew that the church holding the sword can be a very dangerous thing. The church is not to violate that separation by picking up the sword, such as the Romans did.

Another example of this comes from the story of King Uzziah of Israel. King Uzziah was a great and generous king of Israel. It was said he was blessed with many victories in battle and ample blessings in times of peace. King Uzziah was a great respecter of the Almighty, until he broke the separation of God's ordainment. II Chronicles 26: 16-20 tells us the story.

16 But after Uzziah became powerful, his pride led to his downfall. He was unfaithful to the Lord his God, and entered the temple of the Lord to burn incense on the altar of incense. 17 Azariah the priest with eighty other courageous priests of the Lord followed him in. 18 They confronted King Uzziah and said, "It is not right for you, Uzziah, to burn incense to the Lord. That is for the priests, the descendants of Aaron, who have been consecrated to burn incense. Leave the sanctuary, for you have been unfaithful; and you will not be honored by the Lord God." 19 Uzziah, who had a censer in his hand ready to burn incense, became angry. While he was raging at the priests in their presence before the incense altar in the Lord's temple, leprosy broke out on his forehead. 20 When Azariah the chief priest and all the other priests looked at him, they saw that he had leprosy on his forehead, so they hurried him out. Indeed, he himself was eager to leave, because the Lord had afflicted him.

This seems to be a very stark message to the powers of government, that the government is not to impose on anything the church does. King Uzziah wanted to enter the holy temple with the priests and burn incense. The priests, aware of God's ordainment, told him no, to turn around and let them fulfill that role. The king ignored the priests' warnings and God struck him with leprosy. God enlightened to us that the church is not to take up the sword and the government is not to take any action inside the church.

This is also a prime example that "war against poverty" or other government welfare programs such as food stamps and socialized medicine, while administered with good intentions, will never be able to properly raise the less fortunate out of poverty. God charged the Church with fulfilling this action and it is the Church's responsibility to take up that cross. More specifically, it is our responsibility as Christians to faithfully tithe and give our churches the ability to fulfill that role. Government issuing programs to help the poor will only result in debt, dependence and greater need. These social welfare programs will not work because they do not make sense Biblically. When something doesn't make sense Biblically, it is branded for failure economically.

Now that we have a better understanding of the separation of church and state, and where it comes from, we need to look at how it has been used against the establishment of religion in our nation. In 1876 the American Liberal Union was the first entity that declared our nation's founding was based on secularism. It took years and years as it often does, but as a great phycologist once said, "No matter how absurd the lie, if you repeat it often enough, people will believe it.". In the 1930s and 40s textbooks began to be rewritten proclaiming our founding fathers were deists and all mentions of religion were removed from our founding fathers' quotes. The modern books resembled a block of Swiss cheese, considering how many facts had to be removed, but once again, if you keep saying it, people will believe it.

By 1947 the supreme Court took up a case known as Everson vs. the Board of Education. The court stated, "The 1st amendment has erected a wall of separation between church and state. That wall must be kept high and impregnable."[26] This court case decided that it was unconstitutional for Christian parents, sending their children to private Christian schools to receive tax breaks, considering their children were not putting any burden on the public-school system. However, the supreme Court couldn't have the government giving tax breaks to anything that had to do with religion because of the "separation of church and state" phrase. The court refused to read Jefferson's intent in his letter to the Danbury Baptists and proceeded to flip all precedence to where government would now be hostile to the establishment of religion.

---

[26] Everson v. Board of Education, 330 U.S. 1, 18 (1947)

On June 25th, 1962 we also witnessed the further dissent against Christianity as school prayer was struck down by the Engel vs. Vitale case.[27] This case was especially detrimental to the cause of religious freedom because it changed the language as to what the government believes the word "church" means. For 120 years the definition of "church" had been defined as a federally established denomination. Not Baptist, not Catholic, Episcopalian, but as "church" only. The court case changed the definition to reflect that "church" was to be known as any public display of religious activity. That now meant the government had control over our nativity scenes, public prayer and displays of the Ten Commandments on public grounds. It's astounding how far America has come from where she was.

A short list of supreme Court cases involving the separation phrase

Stone v. Graham, Ring v. Grand Folks Public School District (1980) – Unconstitutional for students to see the Ten Commandments displayed in school considering they might read, meditate upon, respect or obey them.

Harvey v. Cobb County (1993) – Removed Ten Commandments from County Court houses.

Harris v. Joint School District (1994)– When a student addresses an assembly of his peers he is effectively

---

[27] Engel v. Vitale, 370 U.S. 421 (1962)

a representative of the government and it is unconstitutional for that student to engage in prayer.

Roberts v. Madigan (1990) – Unconstitutional for a school library to contain books dealing with Christianity. It is also unconstitutional for a teacher to be seen with a personal library at a public school.

Ohio v. Whisner (1976) – Unconstitutional for any board of education to use the word "God" in any official writings.

Flory v. Sioux Falls School District (1979) – Unconstitutional for anyone to discuss whose birthday we celebrate on Christmas with kindergarteners.

Because a prosecuting attorney mentioned seven words from the Bible, a statement that lasted less than five seconds, a jury sentence was overturned for a man that clubbed a 71-year-old woman to death.[28]

In Defuniak, Florida, a judge ordered the courthouse copy of the Ten Commandments be covered up during a murder trial lest the words, "Thou shalt not kill" allow the jury to be prejudiced against the defendant.[29]

---

[28] Commonwealth v. Chambers; 599 A. 2D 630, 643-644 (Sup. Ct. Pa. 1991), *cert denied*, case no. 91-1597, May 26th, 1992, petition for rehearing denied August 18th, 1992

[29] *Olean Times Herald*, Monday, April 6th, 1992, p. A-1; see also *State of Florida v. George t. Broxson,* Case No. 90-02930 CF (1st Jud. Cir. Ct. Walton County, Fl., 1992)

So in looking at these instances of the supreme Court ruling against religious freedoms and conservatism, how do we turn this back?

Chapter 8
Activism

If we look back to the story of Moses in Numbers, you may remember the event with Moses and the stone. God told Moses to go speak to the stone and Moses goes with Aaron to the stone, and asks "Do I really have to get water for you again?" and strikes the stone twice.

Numbers 20:10-12 illustrates the story. *10 "Then Moses and Aaron gathered the assembly together before the rock, and he said to them, "Hear now, you rebels: shall we bring water for you out of this rock?" 11 And Moses lifted up his hand and struck the rock with his staff twice, and water came out abundantly, and the congregation drank, and their livestock. 12 And the Lord said to Moses and Aaron, "Because you did not believe in me, to uphold me as holy in the eyes of the people of Israel, therefore you shall not bring this assembly into the land that I have given them."*

Was Moses the only one that suffered God's punishment? Let's look back at the passage. God doesn't just address Moses but also tells Aaron that he cannot go to the promised land. Aaron's silence and inactivity prompted the judgment of an entire nation. Just as Aaron and the people of Israel were held accountable, so are we. We look up to God and shrug our shoulders saying there's nothing we can do. We moan that our leaders are corrupt, that they do not follow God's will. However, God looks at us in return as He did at Aaron and holds us accountable in the same way. Christians suffer for our inactivity. Proverbs 24:11 reveals a moral obligation to do something, *"Deliver those who are drawn toward death, and hold back those stumbling towards the slaughter."*

Submitting to Authority

Some Christians will sight Romans 13 as a reason not to challenge authority. I would call it an excuse, but nonetheless, there are Jesus followers taking God's word out of context when it comes to challenging government authority. The words of Romans 13 can easily be misconstrued as an excuse to not stand against tyranny. It reads *13 "Let everyone be subject to the governing authorities, for there is no authority except that which God has established. The authorities that exist have been established by God."*

We must realize, once again, that God ordained three structures in our lives, the church, our family and government. This was God ordaining the institute of government and telling us that there should be laws and they should be obeyed. This verse is warning against the evils of anarchy. God is saying that there needs to be a structure in society for his people to flourish. He's not telling us that we cannot change our government or nullify certain laws. He's instructing that a structure of government is needed. This verse had been directed towards the Zealots of Biblical times. There was a group of Jews, led by Simon the Zealot, that did not pay taxes, did not abide by the laws and had no interest in doing so. God, in His wisdom, realized that this would turn into the Church taking on the role of government and rebuked the practice with the words from Romans 13.

The Dangers of Single Issue Advocacy

In my time in the field of activism I've seen several groups of people who specialize on one singular issue. They take an issue, learn everything there is to know about it and hammer that issue home. Among the subjects that tend to be focused in on as single issues are the 2nd Amendment, pro-life and traditional marriage debates. It's very important to have people educating themselves and being the subject matter experts when it comes to their issue of passion. However, we've seen the church be fooled more than once when they decide to base their votes on just one single issue. When we do this, it makes it very easy for politicians to drum up votes based on an issue they could care little about or maybe not even support.

Don't misunderstand, we need subject matter experts on all different kinds of issues across the board. This gives us leaders who can champion certain fights, rally more people to the cause and be effective in getting legislation passed. The danger I'm speaking of is when church bodies or individuals decide they will support a candidate based on just one issue. If a candidate says he is pro-life but isn't fiscally conservative when it comes to budgetary matters, they can be just as destructive to liberty and God's Law as a liberal leftist. We must realize that if someone votes pro-life but at the same time votes to allow secular and even sinful materials to be taught to our children in public schools, the pro-life vote they cast doesn't amount to anything when the next generation is being told that gender is fluid or that our founding fathers were deists. The warning is this: just because a politician says they support an issue you're passionate about, doesn't mean they can't indirectly work to undermine that issue. Over taxation and the 2nd amendment have just as much to do with morality as pro-life and sanctity of marriage issues. We must be educated across the board on numerous issues that affect us and our children's future. From immigration, to global warming, to gun rights, to taxes, we must have a firm grasp on what we believe and then if we want to become the subject matter expert on one subject, we can go champion that and lead others.

From What I've Learned…

Now that you want to get involved (you do want to get involved right?) we must find a way to channel that energy in an effective way. Not everything you do in the realm of politics will be considered productive. I've been there, and I've found out what is and isn't productive and it's important to spend your time and resources wisely.

In the world of politics, it's easy to come into situations where rivalries and miniscule arguments over personalities eclipse the real goal of furthering conservatism. When going to your first meetings, keep an eye out for fights over personalities vs fights over principles. We're here to fight for principles, not fight over which club or group has more people or puts on better events. Keep your eyes on being focused on making a difference. How do we do this?

First of all, when being asked to volunteer for something, try to see how it will benefit the movement. Should you go and help bake cookies for the GOP bake sale, or should you opt for making phone calls and going door to door to talk to voters? I would automatically opt for the latter. In many cases, a non-profit organization or a citizen's group can be more effective in making a lasting difference than just lining the coffers of a political group's fundraising needs. Of course, everything I'm saying here is very broad and you will have to make the ultimate decision of how your time is best spent. Listen to people talk when at meetings. When they say they are against someone or a candidate, find out if it's over personality or principle.

There are far too many political groups out there that have the same goals but because of personalities, or an inability to get along, or maybe even a mishap from 10 years ago they focus on personal feuds instead of principled stands. Find a group that is united in its cause.

I would advise to exercise caution when jumping right into political party meetings. When first getting involved one can be quickly turned around in the chaos of party politics. Just because everyone in the room claims to be a Republican does not mean they are on the same side. I've seen political meetings that have been just as divisive as if half the room were liberals and the other half were conservatives. I'm not advising not to go to party meetings but make sure you have your sea legs before jumping in. I've seen several aspiring activists come into a party meeting and go right back out based on some of the bickering over personalities, never to be seen again. After you've spent some time familiarizing yourself with the issues and have garnered a decent volunteer base to rally with you, then you can storm the party meetings but be ready for a fight. Establishment types have a special hatred for new blood.

On another note, just to make sure you yourself don't get sucked into personality politics, never sign onto a candidate or leader because you like them, they're your friend, or if they shook your hand and complimented your attire. I have friends I wouldn't vote for, and you should to! Just because someone is a good person, they go to your church or made an impressive speech at your last meeting does not mean you shouldn't break formation with them if they stray away from your principles. Political loyalty over celebrity, status or even friendship is a very dangerous thing. Our allegiance is not to any one person, politician or leader. It is to Natural Rights and the God that gave them. So don't start carrying the water for a candidate, be a torch bearer for the principles you stand for. As long as any candidate is following by your example, they'll be worth working for, as long as they adhere to the values that proclaim conservatism.

Chapter 9

A Call to Arms

Imagine, if you would, a room full of people, 22 people to be exact. Some of the people are clothed in rags, and a few of the people are clothed in lavish outfits. Most of the people look tired, hungry or malnourished. Some look oppressed, as though they have been beaten down and neglected. Sad faces of hunger and distrust permeate the crowd and seem to represent the majority of the group. Just a very select few appear as though they are enjoying the health of a full stomach and a roof over their heads. After a close look however, you notice that everyone in this room is sitting, except for one. There is something different about this one person standing among the 22. His head is held higher, his clothes in better condition, his demeanor more confident. There is a different atmosphere about this man; an atmosphere of creativity, self-worth, and virtue. If this entire room were to represent the population of the world, this one man standing would be an American.

The wonderful thing about this illustration is, if you are reading this and currently reside in America, you are the one in 22 people who are blessed to live in the "shining city on a hill" as Ronald Reagan so frequently referred to America. Only one in 22, that's it! How does that make you feel? Is it not amazing that you were picked by our Creator out of every 22 people to live here? What kind of odds have we surmounted to be blessed to not live in a third world country, to not live under oppression, to not live in a society where instead of wondering what movie we'll see next, we're wondering where our next meal will come from? Is it not true that to be picked, one out of 22, is not only miraculous but does also foretell of an important and meaningful life? Ask yourself; why would God bless you to live here if you're just an average person with no plan or purpose?

The answer is; He does have purpose for you! Considering we were one picked out of many He expects us to carry out that plan!

We must also remember that being selectively chosen will mean great challenges, much like we are seeing today. We struggle with the malicious intent of liberals and the media; we face propaganda and lies about us, however, regardless of all the shots taken at us, we remain that one in 22. Many of us struggle with that overwhelming feeling that America is gone forever, and we can't fight what's going on; however, we've overcome bigger odds because we're one in 22. We struggle with the feeling that the challenges are enormous, and victory seems unlikely, however, we are one in 22!

In being, as I believe, selected, no grander responsibility could have been levied upon us than to protect the inalienable rights given to us by Providence! Given this statistic, it is in my opinion that the predetermined duty of all Americans is to come forth and be patriots for our God and country, upholding the Constitution and the Bible.

So far Americans have three things outlined here:

1. An Immense Amount of Privilege – Day by day remember how blessed you are and thank God.
2. A Wall of Challenges – God picked the one out of 22 He could use; the one that would be able to rely on Him to face these challenges.
3. A Massive Responsibility – Next time you don't want to have that uncomfortable conversation with someone who disagrees with you, or next time you don't want to show up to volunteer on a campaign or at church, or the next time you just don't feel like being the light in the darkness, remember, God's counting on you to do so because someone else could be where you are, doing what you won't do.

The next time it seems like all is lost and America is helpless just remember, "Hey…I'm one in 22."

"All that is necessary for evil to succeed is for good men to do nothing."

Truer words were never spoken. There is a call going out to the church to do something about the state of our country. Many pastors refuse to bring up politics because it might offend someone. When the survival of our country hangs in the balance, it may just be time for someone to be offended. Here's the danger of the narrative the progressive left has been pushing, because now, even Christians believe it! The pastors have accepted separation of church and state not only in society but within the own walls of the church. Martin Luther King noted, *"There was a time when the church was very powerful. It was during that period when the early Christians rejoiced when they were deemed worthy to suffer for what they believed. In those days the church was not merely a thermometer that recorded the ideas and principles of popular opinion; it was a thermostat that transformed the mores of society. Wherever the early Christians entered a town the power structure got disturbed and immediately sought to convict them for being "disturbers of the peace" and "outside agitators" ... They brought an end to such ancient evils as infanticide and gladiatorial contest."*

Now we wonder why politicians may pander to the center when what we want is a true conservative in office. Now I do want to beg the question, "Could it be that those to the left and center are so much more involved than we are, that politicians see no need to try to earn our votes?"

In this book we've gone over many stories of the founder's faith and how they implemented it. Now the question must be answered...What will it take?

Our Bible says clearly in 2 Chronicles 7:14, *If my people who are called by my name, shall humble themselves and pray, and seek my face, and turn from their wicked ways; then will I hear from heaven, and will forgive their sin, and will heal their land."*

If we believe this to be true, we should take all courses of action in this verse. Too many Christians read this verse with only the prayer being used to turn our nation around. When we are saved not only do we pray but we take action by turning from our wicked ways and embracing the ways of our Lord, to better our lives and our walk with him. However, when it comes to our country we seem to stop at that first clause. We pray, but for our faith to be genuine we must also make priority to *turn* from the sin of disengagement in our government. In this verse God tells us to pray. God also tells us to humble ourselves, seek His face and turn from our ways. For every one instance of prayer we see in this verse, we see three instances of action. This should tell us that prayer is important, and action is where change can be manifested.

John Hancock, in writing the numerous prayer proclamations he issued realized the need for Christian activism. *"I urge you by all that is dear, by all that is honorable, by all that is sacred, not only that ye pray but that ye act."*

President Theodore Roosevelt wrote in his book, "Fear God and Take Your Own Part", *"But in addition to fearing God, it is necessary that we should be able and ready to take our own part. The man who cannot take his own part is a nuisance in the community, a source of weakness, an encouragement to wrongdoers and an added burden to the men who wish to do what is right. If he cannot take his own part, then somebody else has to take it for him."* The more I involve myself with what's going on out there, the more I begin to understand, that we are no longer fighting a battle of left vs. right, democrat vs. republican, progressive vs conservative. We are fighting a battle of good vs. evil. Many good men have laid down their lives so that we can participate or choose not to.

Looking back on the blood that has been spilled for this country, the sacrifice is truly astounding. To see and hear about the pain, the anguish, the sacrifice of others who came before us, that's what motivates me to knock on doors, make phone calls and seek knowledge regarding our political system. It's hard to understand the losses so many have been through death and sickness. Some dying on the battle fields still in their teens, with hardly any life having been lived. Some receiving that knock on the door from a man in uniform to tell the grave news of a lost loved one. Some clenching the letters or pictures from back home as they drew their last breaths for freedom's sake on the battlefield. When we think about the forfeiture of life for our sakes, it's apparent just how easy we have it. We don't have to storm the beaches of Normandy. We don't have to slosh through the trenches of France. We don't have to bandage our bloodied, shoeless feet marching to Trenton on Christmas morning. We merely have to raise our voices, volunteer, organize and just be engaged with our communities. Some people act as though political activism is some unbearably heavy burden, but have they taken the time to really think about what unbearable weights others have carried, just for us to have the freedom not to care? I find myself wondering are we worth it? Are you and I worth their sacrifice? Is our salt and light tasteful and bright enough to be worth a mother losing her son, a son losing his dad, a brother losing his brother? Have we earned our keep? Have we pulled our weight back here at home? Are we vigilant in knowing that the country they are fighting for is worth dying for?

Our society has become so preoccupied with work, games, tv, entertainment, music and sports, that the thought of political activism seems overwhelmingly boring. People complain about the mail they get in their mailboxes around election time, the phone calls they receive. People who are fed up with politics and don't want anything to do with it. We hear from people who complain about the state of our country, the taxes, the economy but it's hard not to ask, "what are you doing about it?" We wonder why our nation has come under such leftist, big government rule that seeks to stifle our voices, our freedoms, our Christianity. We wonder how it is that we live in a country where babies can be aborted right up until the last minute and have their body parts sold for profit. The answer? Because we let them. We wonder why we live under a government that allows the imprisonment and legal persecution of Christians displaying their faith. The answer? Because we let them. We wonder why we have a power structure of elitist politicians that say marriage is no longer an institute of the church but of the government. We wonder why they corrupt and twist the sanctity of marriage. The answer? Because we let them. Why do we have government ripe with runaway spending, debt and corruption? The answer? Because we let them. Do you think it's time we stop letting them do this? Do you believe as I do, that you and I have a moral, Biblical obligation, and ordainment to be politically active?

I'm so glad you have taken the time to read this book and discover the truth of our nation's birth. Education is the foundation of making a change. There's just one more step, and that is to get politically active. Let's read an excerpt from Patrick Henry's address to the Second Virginia Convention on March 23, 1775, at St. John's Church in Richmond, Virginia. Note the fervor and passion this man felt in his heart to go give up everything for freedom's sake.

"They tell us, sir, that we are weak; unable to cope with so formidable an adversary. But when shall we be stronger? Will it be the next week, or the next year? Will it be when we are totally disarmed, and when a British guard shall be stationed in every house? Shall we gather strength by irresolution and inaction? Shall we acquire the means of effectual resistance, by lying supinely on our backs, and hugging the delusive phantom of hope, until our enemies shall have bound us hand and foot? Sir, we are not weak if we make a proper use of those means which the God of nature hath placed in our power. Three millions of people, armed in the holy cause of liberty, and in such a country as that which we possess, are invincible by any force which our enemy can send against us. Besides, sir, we shall not fight our battles alone. ...The battle, sir, is not to the strong alone; it is to the vigilant, the active, the brave...

There is no retreat but in submission and slavery! Our chains are forged! Their clanking may be heard on the plains of Boston! The war is inevitable²and let it come! I repeat it, sir, let it come.

It is in vain, sir, to extenuate the matter. Gentlemen may cry, Peace, Peace²but there is no peace. The war is actually begun! The next gale that sweeps from the north will bring to our ears the clash of resounding arms! Our brethren are already in the field! Why stand we here idle? What is it that gentlemen wish? What would they have? Is life so dear, or peace so sweet, as to be purchased at the price of chains and slavery? Forbid it, Almighty God! I know not what course others may take; but as for me, give me liberty or give me death!"- Patrick Henry[30]

The founding fathers knew that adherence to natural law would keep us from diving into societal upheaval, so they embedded it into every corner, every fabric of our design as a nation. Let's fill those shoes once again. Let's take up that torch. Let's say to the forces of evil that no such darkness shall impede upon God's country if the virtuous people of America can stand in that doorway with the light of conservatism, shining bright and cutting through the darkness of government control. Let us say that our government is not our god, not because we feel that way but because we know deep down, that we've done our part in protecting so precious an article as freedom. I

---

[30] History.org. (2017). *Patrick Henry's "Give Me Liberty Or Give Me Death" Speech.* [online] Available at: http://www.history.org/almanack/life/politics/giveme.cfm [Accessed 30 Dec. 2017].

beg of you, at the benefit of those bearing the weight of public activism, we need your help! We need your voice! We need your presence! This next decade I'm sure we will see persecution of conservative ideals, Christian families and traditional values. However, even though we walk through the valley of the shadow of death we will fear no evil.

God has given this country what it has been so long asking for, not from the actions of the left but from the inaction of His people. For all that tyranny needs to grab a foothold is for men of good conscious to remain silent. As it reads in Psalms 30 verse 5, "For his anger is but for a moment, and his favor is for a lifetime. Weeping may tarry for the night, but joy comes with the morning." For the next decade of darkness, we are about to enter the long struggle of working for that morning light, that restoration of the shining city on a hill, for that nation that brings forth the fruit of men and bears blessings from God almighty.

I also want to warn you that Satan will lay any excuse, any reason, any distraction in front of you to keep your influence at bay. Satan understands better than we do just how much of an influence you could have on the tool he has used for centuries to persecute God's people. Satan will tell you things like, "You're not the kind of person to lead anyone. You're not the type to just call up people. You don't know about issues. Those people don't want to hear what you have to say." Satan will also tell you "Well, you just haven't been called to this. Let others take care of it who are more capable." Maybe Satan is also reminding you of that one thing in your past that keeps popping back up as a reminder of failure. Maybe he's using that to give you doubt in your qualifications. We must remember that God doesn't call the qualified. He qualifies the called! Imagine being Moses! Moses, a man with a terrible stutter, was told to go speak to a king; to not only speak to him but threaten him! It's difficult to imagine the bravery and faith it took to do that, and yet, we're nervous about calling someone over the phone or knocking on someone's door.

God told us to "occupy until I come", He wasn't speaking about occupying just the church or just our homes, He meant everywhere, and now one of the most important places He had in mind has been taken over by a progressive, secular movement that seeks to remove morality and religion at every opportunity. Without activism we will leave the leaders of the conservative movement to be crushed under the heavy hand of government. What say you? Will we continue to pray that somehow virtuous Christian leaders will be elected without the activism of other Christians? Or will we gird our loins and take charge of the responsibilities God has handed us?

I truly hope some of these stories have stirred your soul and have empowered you to know that the change we all seek in our nation resides within you! And in conclusion let's look at a pamphlet that a brave, starving, freezing group of men heard from the east side of the Delaware river on December 23rd, 1776.

There are hundreds of men desperately trying to cross the Delaware, dragging with them food, munitions and even cannons across a river heavily congested with ice. Communications have broken down and two other regiments who were instructed to cross at different locations upon the river have been blocked from advancing, leaving Washington's men alone to face the British in nearby Trenton. All seems for naught, but our heroes press on against the bitter cold darkness. In the slow lumbering process of crossing the ice choked river, hooves can be heard galloping through the darkness and getting closer. From the cold night, a lone rider emerges, riding up to General Washington a pamphlet in his hand, just off the presses. Washington takes it, reads as much as he can from the waning moonlight and returns it to the deliverer. The courier, instructed to read it aloud to the freezing men began with these words from Thomas Pain. *"These are the times that try men's souls. The summer soldier and the sunshine patriot will, in this crisis, shrink from the service of their country; but he that stands by it now, deserves the love and thanks of man and woman. Tyranny, like hell, is not easily conquered; yet we have this consolation with us, that the harder the conflict, the more glorious the triumph. What we obtain too cheap, we esteem too lightly: it is dearness only that gives everything its value. Heaven knows how to put a proper price upon its goods; and it would be strange indeed if so celestial an article as FREEDOM should not be highly rated"*[31]

[31] Ushistory.org. (2017). *Thomas Paine: American Crisis*. [online] Available at: http://www.ushistory.org/paine/crisis/c-01.htm [Accessed 30 Dec. 2017].

In closing, I want you to remember that when someone asks you to go to a tea party meeting or a county council session or to go knock on doors or make phone calls for something or someone you believe in, they're not asking you to die for your country like so many have. They're asking you to LIVE for it, like so few will.

About the Author

Tommy Dimsdale was born and raised in Spartanburg, SC. From his late teens to now he has found a significant passion in political activism.

Growing up, his uncle, Gary Poole, would often listen to 106.3 word at a family glass business. As Tommy grew older he would listen more intently, hearing about the serious problems of the nation. In 2010 he went to his first Tea Party meeting and realized his calling to influence the world of politics. Working alongside numerous campaigns, PACs, and advocacy groups for over eight years, Tommy saw a vacancy of Christian and youth activists in the Conservative movement. After previously running a weekly podcast show, The Dimsdale Debate, and serving as the Spartanburg County GOP Secretary, Tommy decided to turn towards speaking at churches and youth group gatherings to drum up activism and share with Christians the answers to lies from the secular liberal left. He most enjoys hosting classes on Christian activism and loves teaching youth classes to high schoolers, ready to embark on their journey through college. Tommy continues to promote activism across the state of South Carolina and works as a real estate agent.